VICTORIA
British Columbia

PUBLISHED BY:
NATURAL COLOR PRODUCTIONS
#17, 1610 DERWENT WAY, DELTA,
NEW WESTMINSTER,
BRITISH COLUMBIA.
V3M 6W1

Copyright 2001 by:
Natural Color Productions
#17, 1610 Derwent Way, Delta
New Westminster, B.C.
V3M 6W1
Telephon: (604) 521-1579
Fax: (604) 522-0145
Victoria: (250) 478-1995

Edited by Diane Johnston

Photo Editing by Brad Nickason

Design by Brad Nickason
Nickason Illustration and Design
Phone (604) 540-0226

Printed and bound in Singapore

CANADA CATALOGUING
IN PUBLICATION DATA

ISBN: 1-895155-05-3

VANCOUVER
ISLAND

BRITISH
COLUMBIA

VANCOUVER

ISLAND

VANCOUVER

BELLINGHAM

VICTORIA

PACIFIC
OCEAN

U. S. A.

Above: This unique photo of Victoria's inner harbour from the air features the Empress Hotel and the Royal British Columbia Museum.

A centrepiece attraction in Victoria is the provincial Legislature. Designed by Francis Rattenbury, a master architect of the late nineteenth century, this superb structure opened in 1898. Statues of famous British Columbians, including Sir James Douglas, the founder of Victoria, are in the inner rotunda where larger-than-life murals portray the drama of B.C.'s history. The wrought-iron gate at the Main Entrance was brought from London, England but most of the materials were quarried or mined right here in coastal areas of B.C.. Free tours are available daily.

Above: Dogwood blossoms, official emblem of British Columbia.

Right: The B.C. Legislative Building front entrance.

Hanging flower baskets, white global cluster street lamps and beautifully made vessels of many descriptions tell you right away that this is no ordinary city. Welcoming visitors has been an integral part of Victoria's heritage for the past century. (Commissioned by the Canadian Pacific Railway and designed by Rattenbury, The Empress Hotel has offered opulent

elegance to many travellers since it opened in 1908.) The famous street lamps first appeared in 1913 and have since become one of its trademarks. So, too, have the cascades of colourful blossoms of the hanging flower baskets.

Bottom left: Hundreds of master crafted classic boats converge on the Inner Harbour for the Classic Boat Festival.
Top left: Victoria's trademark: a cluster street lamp nested above hanging flower baskets of petunias, marigolds, lobelia and draping nepeta.

Below: A flotilla of classics graces the calm waters of the Inner Harbour.

Upper Right: Street musicians line the Lower Causeway on mild evenings.
Below: Sailboats, fishing boats and lone canoe bask in the amber glow of a Victoria sunset.
Left: A magnificent Arbutus overlooks the harbour.

Victoria is more than just a bit of "Olde England." Contemporary architecture and design blend gracefully with the city's motif. Central to Victoria's identity, water constitutes a predominant theme. Fountains abound in city parks and squares. The sea has carved bays and inlets alongside of which elegant hotels and meandering walkways have been erected. Fisherman's Wharf, just to the right of Laurel Point, attest to yet another facet of a waterfront economy-fishing! Stroll along the shoreline for a glimpse of Victoria's contrasts.

Like a consummate actor, Victoria can wear dramatically different faces with ease. Each part she plays is thoroughly enjoyable and authentic.

Left: Modern-style fountain in Centennial Square beside City Hall.
Below left: Yacht sailing past the Laurel Point Inn.
Right: From float planes to fishing vessels - with the heritage backdrop of Victoria's Old Town.
Below: A study of interesting juxtapositions. Modern next to historical; the opulence of the new Regent Hotel contrasts nicely with the more proletarian fishing boats.

Upper Left: A balmy sunny day on which to celebrate Victoria's 125th Birthday. An open air concert in Beacon Hill Park has drawn a multitude.

Lower Left: Fisgard Lighthouse is the oldest lighthouse on B.C.'s coast. First operated in 1859, it has been restored and is now open to the public daily as a National Historic site.

Upper Right: Harbour seals lounge on rocks in Pedder Bay, a little way west of the City.

Lower Right: The rugged, rocky shoreline of the southwest coast of Vancouver Island is the natural habitat of these California sea lions.

Following Page: Killer whales cavort playfully in the waters alongside the Victoria Golf Club. These Orca whales are the largest member of the Dolphin family and are considered highly intelligent.

The flags of many nations adorn the roof of the Undersea Gardens. Adding to the vast array of colours along Victoria's waterfront, they are proof of the welcome offered to all the world's citizens.

When visiting The Undersea Gardens, scuba divers demonstrate some of the displayed specimens. The anemones are particulary interesting in that they appear to be plants, but have the predatory behaviour of an animal. What wonderful things grow in our oceans.

Above: A rear view of the Legislative Buildings with the Maple Leaf, Union Jack and Royal Ensign flying proudly beside the colorful flag of British Columbia.

Right: The undersea Gardens in Victoria's Inner Harbour exhibits thousands of marine plants and animals in their natural surroundings.

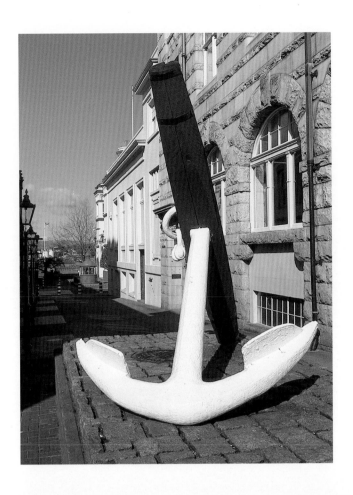

Opposite Page: The Empress Hotel built by the Canadian Pacific Railway Company to ensure their travellers had luxurious accommodation from start to finish on their journeys.
Left: An old anchor alongside the Maritime Museum in Bastion Square.
Below: The Empress Hotel as viewed from across the Inner Harbour.
Following Page: The magnificent evening view of the Legislative Building.

Upper Left: Carr House, on lower Government Street, is the birthplace of Emily Carr. Once thought of locally as "a bit eccentric" her paintings are now prized possessions in private collections and galleries world wide.

Below: Visitors enjoy window shopping in Victoria's many unique stores.

Opposite Page: The Unique entrance to the shopping mall at Market Square.

Victoria exhibits an exciting
cultural diversity.
Nowhere are the contrasts of the
city more apparent than in its vital
downtown core.
The ivied walls of the Empress and
the double-decker London buses,
combined with the nautical flavour
of the docks on the Lower
Causeway, give evidence of our
strong British heritage. The city is
alive with things to do and places
to see.
Many modern and ancient history

exhibits can be seen at the Royal London Wax Museum, containing over 170 life sized figures. Originally designed by Francis Rattenbury as a terminus and ticket office for the Canadian Pacific, this heritage building exhibits the classic design of the Grecian Golden Age.

Further along from the Wax Museum are the ferry docks for the M.V. Coho - which goes between Port Angeles, Washington and Victoria.

Top Left: Visitors stroll around the pedestrian walk on the inner harbour.
Bottom Left: The Wax Museum and Undersea Gardens as viewed across the Inner Harbour.
Below: The elegant architectural lines of the Royal London Wax Museum, grace the south side of Victoria's Inner Harbour.

Top left: The Tally-Ho wagons offer a wonderful way to relax and enjoy the sights of downtown Victoria. They are pulled along by magnificent Clydesdales and Belgians.
Below: The Royal British Columbia Museum provides visitors to Victoria with a look at the history and development of our Province.
Right: Traditional Native Totem Poles in Thunderbird Park across from the Empress Hotel.

Opposite page: Billowing spinnakers against the sky, in the annual Victoria, Swiftsure Yacht Race.
Left: Sailing the scenic waters of the Victoria area offers residents and visitors many opportunities to enjoy the Pacific Coast.
Below: Golfing at the Victoria Golf Club in Oak Bay.

Left: Travelling at an average 28 knots, the ferry Victoria Clipper transports passengers between Victoria and Seattle in 2 1/2 hours.
Below: Over looked by the majestic Empress Hotel Victoria's Inner Harbour is a popular area for visitors and residents alike.

Following Page: The Inner harbour is aglow in the evening lights of the Empress Hotel.

V ictoria's heart and soul can be seen and felt in its waterfront nature. Expansive ocean vistas frame almost all quarters of the city. One of the most beautiful sights is that of Mt. Baker, over 40 miles away near Bellingham, Washington. A not so dormant volcano in the Cascade mountain chain, occasional wisps of steam can be seen like cotton-wool remnants blowing away from its snow-capped cone.

Sheltered from rain by the Olympic Mountains in Washington, and by the Central Mountains of Vancouver Island, Victoria is the sunniest city on Canada's West Coast.

Above: The crimson and gold of maples form an exquisite canopy.
Right: The green pathways along the Dallas Road cliffs form the southern boundary of the city.

When James Douglas first set his eyes on Victoria in 1842, he wrote to a friend: "The place . . . appears a perfect Eden in the midst of the dreary wilderness of the Northwest Coast, and so different is its general aspect . . . that one might be pardoned for supposing it had dropped from the clouds . . ." So enamoured was he that he caused the creation of Beacon Hill Park, established in 1882 as B.C.'s first municipal park.

Exquisite gardens, both formal and wild, winding streams, fountained ponds draped with graceful willows and climbing wisteria can be found throughout the park, as well as a children's petting zoo, playing fields and tennis courts.

Top Left: Rocks, shrubs and the delicate fronds of ferns frame this waterfall in Beacon Hill Park.
Bottom Left: A graceful fountain adorns a duck pond in Beacon Hill Park.
Below: A gorgeous blossoming Dogwood tree graces the lawns at the back of the Legislative Buildings.

A trip to Victoria wouldn't be complete without a visit to the world famous Butchart Gardens. A total delight, they are the inspiration of Mrs. Jennie Butchart who, in 1904, decided to beautify the spent limestone quarry of her husband's cement factory. After hauling in hundreds of tons of soil, and gathering thousands of plant seeds from around the world, she had transformed these 50 acres into a place of joy and beauty. Each season brings a new setting. The lilies and rhododendrons of spring magically become the roses and dahlias of summer. Exquisite Japanese gardens and rockeries please the eye in Fall and Winter. The year round mild climate allows the shrubs and succulents, mass flowers and heathers to create patterns of life throughout the year.

Top Left: Gorgeous hanging baskets, overflowing with colour grace every anteroom, foyer or pathway in the famous Butchart Gardens.
Bottom Left: The Rose Garden and residence.
Top Right: The Italian Garden.
Bottom Right: The Luxurious Private Garden.
Following Page: Cultivated formality, colour and form at Butchart Gardens. Notice the remnant smokestack of the old cement factory in the upper right.

Upper Left: A graceful Arbutus frames the walkway along the Gorge, a finger of salt water that penetrates the city for miles.
Below: A cobalt-blue sky sets off Victoria's trademark hanging baskets.
Right: An enormous bronze statue of Queen Victoria overlooks the harbour of the city that was named in her honour.

"Welcome to Victoria," the garden spells out, and it is truly a wonderful sight for any and all visitors. The enchantingly lit Legislative Buildings dominate this serene evening scene. Sailboats and yachts are nestled in their berths for the night while off in the distance the city's nightlife begins to pulse. The proximity of The Armed Forces in Esquimalt and Colwood makes possible the occasional treat of a military event. These are frequently held on the lawns of the Legislature for all to enjoy.

Above: Naval sunset ceremony on the lawns of the Legislative buildings.
Right: In the heart of Victoria the Inner Harbour welcomes both sea and land going visitors.

When Robert Dunsmir, an ambitious coal-miner from Ayershire, Scotland, embarked on the arduous passage to the new world, in 1851, he promised his bride he would build her a castle. He discovered a rich coal seam near Nanaimo and carefully managed it to become the major coal baron of the Nineteenth Century and one of B.C.'s wealthiest businessmen. He fulfilled his promise with this magnificent structure, built in 1889, which graces a hilltop near downtown Victoria.

His second son, James Dunsmir, was an equally astute man. He became premier of B.C. in 1901, and Lieutenant-Governor from 1906-1909. His home, Hatley Park, was designed by Samuel Maclure and built in 1911. It and the 700 acre Hatley Park estate have become the property of the federal government and now the beautiful pastoral grounds of the Royal Roads Military College.

Top Left: Commandant's Parade at Royal Roads Military College in Colwood, west of the city. Bottom Left: Hatley Castle, now part of Royal Roads Military College. *Below:* Craigdorroch Castle, in the Rockland area of Victoria.

Victoria has enjoyed the elegant fruits of its famous architects. The Legislature, the Empress Hotel and the hundreds of graceful and attractive heritage homes in and around Victoria make it a joy to visit, as well as a special place to live. Stroll through the James Bay and old-Fairfield neighbourhoods and see for yourself.

Upper Right: The Maritime Museum in Bastion Square.
Below: Hatley Castle.
Left: The bronzed imperial grandeur of Queen Victoria graces the lawn of the Provincial Legislature.

The presence of all kinds of water bodies around Victoria, but particularly the ocean, invites athletic events of many types. Rowing, various types of sailing competitions, swimming championships and fishing derbys are ongoing activities. One of the oldest is the Swiftsure Yacht Race. It has been attracting entries from all over the world since 1903. Hundreds of yachts participate in this race in late May of each year. Fishing is an important part of our West Coast economy. Fresh Salmon, Halibut, shrimp and crabs are dietary delights that both visitors and residents enjoy.

Upper Left: A solitary rower sculls off the Gorge on a golden autumn day.
Lower Left: The Annual Swiftsure Race in the Strait of Juan de Fuca.
Right: A Seine fishing vessel in a small harbour near Victoria.
Below: Fishing boats leave Fisherman's Wharf to take their daily catch limits in the seas around the city.
Following Page: Race Rock Lighthouse guards the western approach to Victoria. The magnificent forests and Olympic Mountains of Washington in the background.

Right: The B.C. Ferry, Queen of Vancouver, on the Swartz Bay to Tsawassen run.
Below & Opposite: The B.C. Ferry Corporation operates over 40 ferries which travel between Vancouver Island and mainland B.C.. It is estimated that 16 million visitors travel across the Strait of Georgia to visit Victoria each year.